Balance Amongst the Chaos:
The Daily Journal

This journal is dedicated to those who love making to-do lists and feel satisfied when they are completed. Let's continue to tick off goals, find joy in each day, and create a life we are proud to call our own.

BALANCE AMONGST THE CHAOS

The Daily Journal

Sarah Iaccarino

This Journal Belongs to:

_____

Balance Amongst the Chaos

Sarah Iaccarino

© Sarah Iaccarino 2021

www.healwithaligntherapies.com

aligntherapies.llc@gmail.com

This book is sold with the understanding that the author is not offering specific personal advice to the reader. For professional advice, seek the services of a suitable, qualified practitioner. The author disclaims any responsibility for liability, loss or risk, personal or otherwise, that happens as a consequence of the use and application of any of the contents of this book. This book is not intended as a substitute for the medical advice of physicians. The reader should regularly consult a physician in matters relating to his/her health and particularly with respect to any symptoms that may require diagnosis or medical attention.

All rights reserved. This book may not be reproduced in whole or part, stored, posted on the internet, or transmitted in any form or by any means, electronic, mechanical, photocopying, recording, or other, without permission from the author of this book.

Design and publishing support by www.AuthorSupportServices.com

Illustration on page 282 by Melanie Howarth

ISBN: 9781922375117 Hbk

CONTENTS

Introduction   1

Approaching Mindfulness with an Open Mind & Empty Plate   2

How to Use Your Journal   5

Introducing the Seven Main Chakras   8

What It Means to Manifest Your Desires   13

Adding Intentions to Your Morning Routine   16

Adding Affirmations to Your Daily Self-Talk   19

Incorporating Daily Gratitude   23

A. Connection: Balancing the Root Chakra   29

B. Patience: Balancing the Sacral Chakra   65

C. Confidence: Balancing the Solar Plexus Chakra   101

D. Gratitude: Balancing the Heart Chakra   137

E. Solitude: Balancing the Throat Chakra   173

F. Intuition: Balancing the Third Eye Chakra   209

G. Faith: Balancing the Crown Chakra   245

Closing Letter from the Author   280

One Last Thing...   282

Introduction

The ultimate tool for manifestation, Balance Amongst the Chaos: The Daily Journal is a staple for anyone who has a laundry list of responsibilities and is dedicated to creating a happy, balanced life. This journal teaches you how to implement various manifestation techniques and utilize the Universal energy always available for you. This journal makes manifestation techniques easy to understand so they can be seamlessly implemented into your daily routine. Use this journal as a guide for incorporating spiritual practices as you navigate your busiest days, professional projects, and major life events — you will notice your intentions coming to fruition and your desires unfolding right before your eyes. Offering a personal space to organize daily tasks, set intentions, create affirmations and reflect on your progress, this journal is a key element in self-mastery and will become your most valued possession.

Approaching Mindfulness with an Open Mind & Empty Plate

Everything is changing, constantly. Change is inevitable. The weather changes every season, society continues to develop, and evolution has a never-ending impact on this planet. Just like the earth, your physical body and mind are also evolving, growing slightly older each minute of every day. It is the cycle of life and a major part of human existence. Change is inevitable, but growth is a choice. You have the ability to grow within yourself and evolve with the ever-changing Universe, but it is a conscious decision you must make every day. You cannot stop the change that is consistently occurring internally and externally, but you can grow with it.

The environment you choose to inhabit is a direct reflection of your inner self. This means your thoughts, emotions, and words. You create your world. The Universe unequivocally responds to the energy you exude and has no regard for whether you accept this or not. The concept is simple enough to understand but can be difficult to put into practice. Our minds, controlled by the Ego, instill fear in our bodies, judge ourselves and naturally conjure negative thoughts first. These unavoidably human instincts create resistances; blocking you from living the life you may desire to lead.

When you remove a resistance or energetic block from your life, you allow miraculous events to take place. In short, your prayers will be answered. To release resistances and attract manifestations, it is paramount you align your mindset on the same frequencies as your desires. This is possible with dedication to a structured plan. Consciously shifting your mindset and perspective to an abundant, grateful, and worthy attitude requires consistent implementation of various mindfulness techniques.

'Mindfulness techniques' is an umbrella term covering countless methods, practices and habits developed to help strengthen self-awareness, relax the body and reduce stress. These methods range from breathwork, meditation, yoga, and silent retreats to free writing, intention setting, affirmations, nature walks, remedial massages, listening/playing music, and painting or drawing; along with countless other rejuvenating hobbies. There is a lot to absorb when starting your mindfulness journey, it can feel overwhelming and daunting if you are unsure where to begin. It is important to start small and take one step at a time.

When approaching spirituality and mindfulness techniques, picture yourself at a large buffet with an empty plate. This buffet has a bread section, salad bar, several soup options, rows of entrees offering various cuisines, as well as a dessert station with coffee and tea. The buffet consists of a plethora of mindfulness habits and spiritual practices.

There is an abundance of options to choose from and every option is slightly different from the next. Your plate is empty and you can fill it however you please. Explore all the options and take what you need, looks good and seems appetizing to you at the time. Taste what you've put on your plate and see how you like it. Simply return to the buffet for a second course if you are hungry for more or want to try something new.

Some people will dive into the buffet and fill two plates at once. Some will only have a light salad and a small side. Some skip the whole buffet and go for the coffee and dessert line. Everyone approaches the buffet differently. Maybe you try the same thing every time because you enjoy it, and it works for you. But then, after a few months of experiencing the same thing, you outgrow it and it's no longer as satisfying as it once was. You are yearning to try something new from the buffet — a natural element of human evolution and personal development.

Whichever way you approach the buffet is completely up to you and contingent on your current lifestyle. You can fill your plate with whatever you please. Your plate will look different to the person you're dining with, which is completely fine. What works for you might not work for someone else. Or perhaps you sample a bite of something on your friend's plate and absolutely love it, so you immediately head back to the buffet and grab a serving for yourself. Shared experiences can help you find exactly what you are looking for.

Mindfulness and spirituality are like a buffet, ready for you to fill your plate and sample anything you connect with at the given moment. These practices are intended to make your life easier and more enjoyable. Whatever you are experiencing in life, spiritual and mindfulness practices are designed to bring improvements to your days.

Explore all the options of the mindfulness and spiritual buffet, make sure you try what resonates with your current mental health needs or life goals. Continue to use it if it works for you. Sample something your friend has tried and see if you enjoy it. Keep exploring the buffet until you have built the perfect plate for this stage of your life.

How to Use Your Journal

Use this journal to organize your long list of responsibilities while seamlessly incorporating mindfulness habits into your routine to help manifest your highest desires. Manifesting is the action of creating and shaping an environment to support the achievement of your goals. The foundation of this environment stems from your actions, beliefs, and thought patterns. When your mentality and behaviors are on the same vibrational frequency as your goals then your environment will allow your desires to manifest more quickly, free of energetic resistances. Build the perfect environment for manifestations to flow to you by using mindfulness habits to shape your thought processes and behavioral patterns. Your environment is shaped, and goals are met by consciously choosing to incorporate mindfulness habits every single day.

This journal is designed to help you implement fundamental mindfulness techniques such as intention setting, creating affirmations, daily gratitude list, using Universal energy for guidance, and self-reflection. These habits will help you reach your goals more quickly and add enjoyment to your days by helping you achieve your desires in a pleasant and exciting way. Whatever stage of life you are currently in, there is always room for mindfulness, gratitude, and self-reflection. Whether you are planning your wedding, building a business, finishing your degree, or simply dedicated to becoming a healthier version of yourself, there is an opportunity for self-improvement.

The dates of this journal are blank so you can start using it when called to begin your mindfulness journey. You do not have to wait until Monday, the first of the month or January to start. Furthermore, the blank dates allow for mental health breaks without needing to remove any excess pages. Perhaps you take every Sunday off to enjoy time with family or maybe you need a week-long holiday from all commitments to mentally regroup. Whenever you are ready to jump back into the grind, your journal will be ready with a blank page to guide you in bringing mindfulness and balance into your chaotic life.

You are holding a blank slate and it is yours to utilize in whichever way you see fit. Personalize it with your long-term goals, any fears, doubts or negative habits you wish to overcome, daily inspiration, and moments of success. Just like your life, you can build it to look however you like. Use this journal to create the life and mindset you aspire to have.

Each page is designed to encourage intention setting, create personal affirmations and write a daily gratitude list. At the conclusion of each page, there is space for self-reflection to be completed at the end of your day. This segment highlights the biggest wins and lessons that occurred throughout your day; a crucial factor in reaching long-term goals and bringing your desires to fruition. Your behaviors and actions need to match your intentions if you wish to reach your goals — simple as that. It is important to hold yourself accountable for adhering to the intentions you set and reflect on your progress towards them. If your actions and behaviors do not match your intentions, then you might as well not set any. Establish the life you wish to lead, write your intentions, write your affirmations, express gratitude and raise the frequency of your actions and behaviors to match the same frequency of the new intentions you have set. Watch and feel yourself transform each day; you will achieve your goals sooner than expected.

Throughout this journal, there are seven topics of behaviors used to encourage self-reflection through journal prompts. These behaviors are associated with the main chakra system, which is summarized at the beginning of the journal. (If you are seeking an advanced explanation of the chakra system and further your understanding of the role they sustain in wellness, you are encouraged to purchase your own copy of *Balance Amongst the Chaos: Your Step-by-Step Guide to Wellbeing*

Through the Chakras.) These journal prompts create an opportunity for authentic self-reflection and evaluation of your current behavioral patterns, emotional blocks, or fear-based resistances that hinder any progress towards your current goals/intentions. Free-write and answer the journal prompts that complement your current mental and physical needs. These prompts are here for any moment calling you to delve into your human psyche and explore your habits.

Lastly, and undoubtedly the most important, use Universal energy to help make your days easier and more balanced — you cannot do everything by yourself, and you do not have to. Write a daily to-do list for the Universe and give them tasks to complete to make your list smaller. It is here to support you throughout all your endeavors. Open yourself to the energies surrounding you, pass off the tasks you need help with, and allow the Universe to work with you.

Remember, this life is meant to be enjoyed. Make room for play, creativity, and laughter as you build the life of your dreams. These small habits will help you achieve balance, joy and inner peace — even on your most chaotic days.

Introducing the Seven Main Chakras

The chakras are centers of invisible energy in the human body keeping you lively, vibrant, and balanced every day. Every human being currently lives with their own chakra system, and the innate ability to activate it. Chakras are not contingent on age, gender, socioeconomic status, or cultural background. We all have them. This similarity connects us to one another on a mental, physical, and spiritual level. Regardless of your conscious awareness of chakras, they still exist in your body and directly impact your mental and physical wellbeing.

Chakras transfer and store energy throughout the entire human body and are responsible for the functionality and vitality of one's physical, mental and emotional health. Each chakra plays a separate, yet significant, role in each dimension of wellness, through representing a spiritual life lesson, depicting a common emotional challenge, and signifying a certain component of wellness in need of healing. Resulting from the chaotic world we live in, energy can become blocked in a certain chakra, creating an energetic resistance and imbalance. These imbalances appear as physical and psychological symptoms resulting from a diagnosed illness, traumatic life experience, emotional burden, physical injury, or societal conditioning.

A clear understanding of each chakra and the influence they have on behavioral patterns illuminates the challenges one must overcome to strengthen the connection between body and spirit and create a life they wish to lead. Each chakra can be healed of energetic blockages through self-evaluation and awareness of one's behaviors.

Just as everything is composed and influenced by energetic exchanges, the chakras move at different vibrational frequencies and directly influence the vibration of your physical and emotional body. The chakras vibrate on the same frequency as the body and mind. If you wish to heal, energize, and raise the frequencies of each chakra, you must raise the overall vibration of your body.

The lower three chakras signify survival, creativity, action, and power. The middle chakra, the heart center, signifies compassion and is a gateway between the upper and lower chakras. The upper three chakras vibrate at higher frequencies and signify communication, visualization, and spirituality. Below is a brief overview of the seven main chakras and the role they play in physical, mental and emotional wellness.

Connection

The root chakra emanates a bright red color and is located at the base of the spine, connecting to the adrenal gland. This symbolizes an individual's relationship with themselves and their connection to the earth. Signifying a foundation, it pertains to basic survival needs such as safety, shelter, food, clothing, and a sense of belonging and is blocked by fear and anger. The root chakra can be balanced through grounding exercises that help strengthen the connection to your body and the environment in which you live.

Patience

The sacral chakra radiates an orange aura and is located directly below the belly button, connecting to the gonad gland. When viewing the physical body from head to toe, this chakra is in the exact center. It is connected to the sexual organs and the ability to experience pleasure. The sacral chakra is where an individual expresses their sexuality and creativity but also where feelings of guilt, shame, and insecurities exist, blocking the experience of pleasure. These emotions relate to the nature of relationships and intimate interactions with others. This chakra can be balanced through pelvic floor exercises and delaying gratification through incorporating patience into your daily life — teaching the body and mind to experience and acknowledge emotions before satisfying a craving with a quick fix.

Confidence

The solar plexus chakra is a vibrant yellow color, is located several inches below the chest line, directly above the belly button, and connects to the pancreas gland. This chakra is associated with an individual's personal power and the connection to their community. It influences decision-making ability, image, and personal accountability. It controls one's willpower and is blocked by doubt, shame and insecurity. Ultimately, it connects an individual's self-worth and confidence to the roles they uphold in society. This chakra can be balanced through core exercises and self-esteem practices to strengthen confidence and willpower.

Gratitude

Connected to the thymus gland, the heart chakra emits a deep green color and is located in the center of the chest. This is exceptionally important as it links the higher spiritual chakras with the lower physical ones. It symbolizes altruism, acceptance, and self-love. Additionally, this chakra holds the ability to give and receive forgiveness and is blocked by grief and envy. This chakra can be balanced by forgiving yourself and others, giving before you receive and showing daily gratitude.

Solitude

The throat chakra exudes a turquoise aura and is located at the jugular to control communication. It is connected to the thyroid gland. This pertains to the ability to listen and receive external information as well as honestly articulating thoughts, feelings, and needs. It is associated with an individual's willpower, self-expression and authenticity and is blocked by deception and dishonesty. This chakra can be balanced by resting your voice, taking silent retreats and moments for solitude, and living with authenticity.

Intuition

The third eye chakra is the color of indigo and is located between the eyebrows. It's connected to the pituitary and pineal glands. This chakra creates an attachment between humans and their purpose in the physical world. It poses the questions, "Who am I mentally?" and "What is my vision in life?" It is responsible for the sixth sense, which is the connection to intuition, visualization, discernment, and self-reflection. It is blocked by illusion and obstinance. This chakra can be balanced through meditation practices to strengthen the connection between the emotional body and the physical and mental body. In addition to deepening one's connection to their intuition, the third eye can be balanced by questioning everything you read or hear and thinking for yourself.

Faith

The crown chakra radiates a violet aura and is located at the top of the skull. It links the pineal gland to your higher self. This chakra controls the functions of the brain and central nervous system. It is harnessed to connect to your spirituality and higher power, while also responsible for your level of consciousness, belief systems and enlightenment. It is blocked by attachment and the Ego. This chakra can be balanced by increasing faith, building trust to minimize fear and deepening the connection to your higher self. This occurs through daily prayers and consciously choosing to shift one's perspective from a victim mentality to an abundant mindset in every situation they encounter.

The chakras play a significant role in our everyday life and directly impact our overall wellbeing. The goal of chakra cleansing is to remove blockages by recognizing, managing, and eliminating these symptoms to improve the overall quality of life. Reflect on your behaviors and belief systems because they shape your internal and external environments, directly influencing the vibration of your chakras. Become aware of your thoughts and actions, and everything you feel, think, and speak will manifest into reality.

What It Means to Manifest Your Desires

Manifestation is attracting a desire or something tangible into your existence through belief, attraction and action. Manifesting is another phrase for setting goals and creating an environment to achieve them. It is the product of the teachings of the fourth law of the Universe, The Law of Attraction. This Universal Law states similar entities attract each other. Whatever you wish to achieve (for example financial abundance, career growth, romantic love, material items, or improved physical health) your thoughts, actions, and beliefs need to match your desires. Essentially, manifestation refers to the implementation of various mindfulness strategies and using Universal energy to bring about a personal goal through focusing thought processes and actions upon the desired outcome.

As you start to explore the depth of manifestations, begin by evaluating your current lifestyle. Ask yourself what would bring your life more joy and how could you live a happier more balanced life. Visualize what you would like to attract into your existence to improve your overall wellbeing.

Use these questions as a guide:

- Am I happy with my current physique?
- Does my social circle bring me joy and challenge me?
- Is my partner supportive and complement the lifestyle I aspire to lead?
- Am I happy with my current level of financial income?
- Do I enjoy the city and community I live in?
- Do I feel challenged, appreciated, and valued in my work environment?

- Am I proud of how I utilize any free time?
- Is my home a safe and relaxing sanctuary?

Use these questions to inspire any positive change you would like to bring into your life. Dream about what you would like to manifest to help improve your life.

The most important concept to grasp is that 'manifestation' is not an action. Manifestation is a product — a result of actions taken to achieve something. 'Manifesting' is actively taking steps to create an environment to reach your goals and allow your desires to come to you. Focus your attention and efforts on building the perfect surroundings, and manifestations will flow to you easily.

How do you create the perfect environment for manifestations to occur? Build better habits and raise your vibration by increasing the frequency of your thoughts, emotions and actions. This is what you are doing when you use this journal. You are creating and shaping your environment to allow manifestations to flow to you.

The Law of Vibration states everything — all matter, thoughts, feelings, emotions, and food — has its own specific vibrational frequency. If you wish to attract something positive into your life, your thoughts, feelings, emotions and actions need to match the same frequency of positive desire for it to materialize into your life.

The strength of the frequency depends on the surrounding energy, which can only exist on a matching frequency. Negative thoughts cannot exist in a positive mind. Envy cannot exist in a loving relationship. Idleness cannot exist in a motivated body. Based on the teachings of the 10th Law of the Universe — The Law of Polarity — these negative thoughts, actions, and behaviors do and always will exist. However, it is imperative to be aware of their presence, and consciously choose to remove them from your environment if you wish to manifest your bigger dreams and desires.

When creating the ideal environment for achieving goals and receiving manifestations, focus on your behaviors in the present moment. Perform habits in the present matching the habits of your future self. How will you think, feel and behave when you reach this goal and this manifestation comes to you? Act this way now. This is a key element in raising your vibration. Shifting your mindset, habits, and actions to those your future self would participate in helps bring you closer to your manifestation. If your mindset and habits exist on a lower frequency than your wants and desires, you will struggle to attract the manifestation you are seeking.

Think about what you would like to manifest into your life and write it on the list "What the Universe is Doing" every single day. Inform the Universe and the energies surrounding you what you would like to manifest into your life and then incorporate the appropriate mindfulness practices to shape your environment to allow this manifestation to come to you. Several mindfulness practices that help raise the vibration of your mindset and improve your daily habits are intention setting, affirmations, and expressing gratitude. These practices help shift your mindset from a lacking perspective to an abundant perspective. Implementing these into your daily routine supports the foundation of your new environment and allows manifestations to flow to you more quickly and freely.

Adding Intentions to Your Morning Routine

An intention is a desired thought or statement representing a commitment to following through with future behaviors and actions. It is to bring abstract ideas into your existence. Setting an intention is the act of stating a goal you are determined to accomplish or desiring something to come into your existence through actions and behaviors. It is a commitment made within yourself to improve any area of wellness you are focusing on.

Reflect on your current lifestyle to locate which areas of wellness could benefit from additional attention. Is your financial health suffering because you are socializing every night of the weekend? Are you exercising daily but neglecting any personal commitments and your relationship is hurting as a result? Are you neglecting your professional projects because you spend all your free time watching sports?

Is there room to find a balance between these personal predicaments?

Intentions help us create balance in our lives. Assessing our current lifestyle and accepting where improvements could be made is essential to personal and professional growth. Intentions support the body and mind in finding balance throughout all dimensions of wellness.

Write a daily or weekly intention based on your current emotions and responsibilities. Write this intention at the top of your daily journal page. Start your day with intention and set the tone for how you wish the day to unfold. Achieve this by asking yourself: "What would I like to bring into my life today and this upcoming week?"

Use these questions as a guide:

- Are any dimensions of wellness currently lacking attention? What mindfulness activities would help improve it?
- What emotion am I not experiencing that I wish to?
- What negative habit needs to be removed from my daily life?
- What ritual should I add to my daily routine that will help lift my spirits?
- Do I need guidance on any upcoming decisions? What do I need clarity on?
- What happened today that I need help overcoming, releasing, or accepting?
- What is happening tomorrow that I need support with?

Allow your mind to wander and explore the avenues these questions create. If these questions prompt any thoughts or desires you have about improving your life, keep them at the forefront of your brain and use them to set your daily/long-term goals.

When setting long-term goals, our conscious mind naturally thinks in the future tense. Daily intentions keep our goals focused on the present. They support the embodiment of your future goals by keeping the physical, mental, and emotional body in the present moment. It is impossible to obtain your long-term goals without conscious awareness of your present mentality and behaviors. Your daily intentions build your long-term successes by glorifying your present days.

Daily intentions are a key element in aligning with the environment you are creating to allow manifestations to flow to you. Your environment is a direct relation to the thoughts, actions and beliefs you uphold. Build your environment by setting intentions that match the life you desire.

Your intentions may read:

- I will be more patient with my children and take deep breaths before I respond to any situation.
- I am going to bring my gym bag to work and exercise immediately after leaving the office.
- I plan on reading 50 pages of my new book after dinner.
- I will find and list one positive thing that happens each day.
- I am going to clean my apartment and car and keep it organized.
- I will purchase a water filter and a new water bottle to encourage myself to increase my daily water intake.
- I will eat slowly and truly enjoy each meal I eat today.

Turn your thoughts and intentions into behaviors/actions. After establishing and writing your intention in your daily journal, it is beneficial to speak them aloud. Speaking intentions is exceptionally powerful as it creates extrinsic motivation. After you have spoken your intentions to yourself, repeat these to your partner, accountability buddy, or mentor. You will feel more inclined to follow through with them and incorporate behaviors into your daily routine once they have been written and spoken aloud twice.

Adding Affirmations to Your Daily Self-Talk

Support the manifestation of your intentions through the power of affirmations; these are defined as positive, simple statements declaring specific goals or intentions in their completed state. The purpose of an affirmation is to subtly and consistently convince the mind/body it has already achieved the intended goal. Repetition of affirmations helps reprogram the subconscious mind to remove any doubt and fear around a goal while activating the powers of the Law of Attraction.

These "I am" statements support mental expansion by transforming one's comfort zone. Affirmations help eliminate negative thinking and shift limiting beliefs into confident and certain thoughts. The change in mindset allows space and freedom for one to visualize anything they wish to create or accomplish.

Affirmations help intentions manifest quicker through manipulation of the subconscious mind by shifting the thought process from "I want to have this" to "I am this". Affirmations allow the mind to dream and visualize anything it wants to do, be or become.

Think about the lifestyle you desire, the person you want to be or the character trait you wish to adopt. Shift your language from "I want to be" to "I am".

> Observe how the language evokes different emotions. The *italicized* text represents the desire while the bold text is the affirmation:
>
> - *"I want to be healthier and feel less fatigued."*
> - **"I am healthy and full of energy."**
> - *"I want a passive income. I could do so much more with my time if I had financial freedom."*
> - **"I am so thankful for my passive income. I am grateful for the freedom and abundance I have."**
> - *"I want to be in a happy, healthy, and respectful relationship."*
> - **"I am in the happiest relationship. It feels amazing to share mutual love with someone who brings out my best qualities."**

Affirmations trick the mind into thinking you have already achieved the desire you are looking for. This shifts the frequency of the mind from a mentality of lacking or scarcity to a mindset of abudance. The abundant mindset is where miracles happen, manifestations occur, and prayers are answered. Write an affirmation to match the desire you wish to achieve every morning when setting your daily intention and organizing your to-do list. Embody this affirmation and believe it to be true. This shift in language supports the increase of your body and mind's vibrational frequency to match your desires, allowing your intentions to manifest quicker.

Every morning, evaluate what is on your to-do list and think about a character trait that will help you embody your intentions and complete your responsibilities most successfully. Create an affirmation around this character trait that complements your current desires and intentions. Write it down and speak it aloud.

> **Your affirmations may read:**
> - I am patient.
> - I am strong.
> - I am resilient.
> - I am successful.
> - I am confident.
> - I am wealthy.
> - I am abundant.
> - I am intelligent.
> - I am valued.

Affirmations are designed to help you embody the emotion, desire, and intentions you have set for yourself. Assess your current lifestyle and create an affirmation to match your mental, physical, and emotional needs.

> **Your affirmations may expand to read:**
> - I am a successful business owner.
> - I am a valued employee.
> - I am well-respected and highly regarded for my work.
> - I am confident in my body.
> - I am athletic and a marathon runner.
> - I am healthy and thriving.
> - I am proud of my accomplishments.

- ❀ I am a fantastic parent.
- ❀ I am in a happy and healthy relationship.

Create an affirmation that complements your current environment and what you desire for yourself. Even if you do not quite believe your affirmations yet or have not reached your goals — continue to write and speak an affirmation every day in your journal — as if you have already achieved the trait you wish to embody or the thing you're desiring to attract. It will support you in mentally and physically increasing your vibrational frequency to the same frequency as your desires.

Incorporating Daily Gratitude

Gratitude is a life-changing perspective shift, essential to working with the energies of the Universe. A grateful attitude will guide you to perceive life through the workings of the Universe, allowing you to see the miracles occurring. Gratitude is an emotion as well as an action and is imperative in creating an abundant lifestyle. Whatever you are currently manifesting — financial success, a happy relationship, a beautiful home, or a thriving business — demonstrating grateful behaviors and existing from a space of love helps lessen the gap between you and the manifestation you desire.

Commonly, happiness and gratitude are emotions dependent on achievement or future events or goals. Often, thoughts pervade our mind creating space between our current and future selves. These can cast a judgmental view on our progress, limiting our ability to enjoy the present moment and be proud of our improvement thus far.

We may notice ourselves thinking or saying:

- "I will be content with myself when I lose 10 pounds."
- "I will feel successful when I scale my business to 7 figures."
- "I cannot wait to buy a bigger home. I am sick of this apartment."

Yes, these statements are valid. You will be happy when you reach your goal physique, expand your business, and buy a home. However, a key element to shifting your mindset to allow manifestations to come easily is to be happy and grateful in the present moment. Even though you have not achieved your desired goal, yet. It is crucial to embody gratitude throughout the process as if you have already achieved the goal.

> **Observe how these statements feel in the body compared to those above:**
>
> - "I am blessed to be able to exercise. My body is healthy and functioning and I am grateful for the opportunities to improve myself physically and mentally through exercise."
> - "I am so grateful to be building an income doing what I love. This business impacts so many people and I am looking forward to its expansion so it can improve even more lives."
> - "I love my apartment as it has been the perfect space for this chapter in my life. I am grateful to have the income to afford a mortgage so I can expand my home, family and lifestyle."

Gratitude shifts focus and puts you in a state of abundance. It minimizes fear, enhances faith, makes you feel happier and reminds you of the minor things one might take for granted. Writing and speaking daily gratitude for the things in your life and those you desire increases your frequency and brings you closer to your goals.

Every morning when setting the intention for the day and organizing your to-do list, write a list of things you are grateful for. This will only take five minutes and will positively shift your attitude for the rest of the day. It will help you focus on the beautiful things that exist in your life, taking nothing for granted. When you focus on the things you don't have, your mind becomes darkened by looking for what is wrong and refusing to enjoy life until you receive your desires, thus creating separation from Universal energy.

Your daily gratitude list could read:

- I am thankful for my home and the opportunity to live in a comfortable environment.
- I am grateful for my roommates and the safe living space we have created.
- I am grateful for my partner and the love we share.
- I am thankful for my job and the income it gives me to fund my lifestyle.
- I am grateful for my gym membership and the ability to exercise.
- I am thankful for the opportunity to earn a degree and expand my education.
- I am grateful for my favorite musicians and their music that uplifts my moods.
- I am thankful for this morning cup of coffee.
- I am grateful for the food in my fridge and the clothes on my back.
- I am thankful for my past, present and future clients.
- I am grateful I can freely give energy, love, advice and support to others.
- I am thankful for another day of life.

Be grateful in the present moment and focus your attention on loving the things that you do have, not what you are lacking. Show gratitude for your past, present, and future — observe how your mindset begins to level up to the frequency of your desires and thus, your attitude towards life improves.

"It is not the mountain we conquer, but ourselves."

- Sir Edmund Hillary, the first confirmed Western climber to reach the summit of Mount Everest.

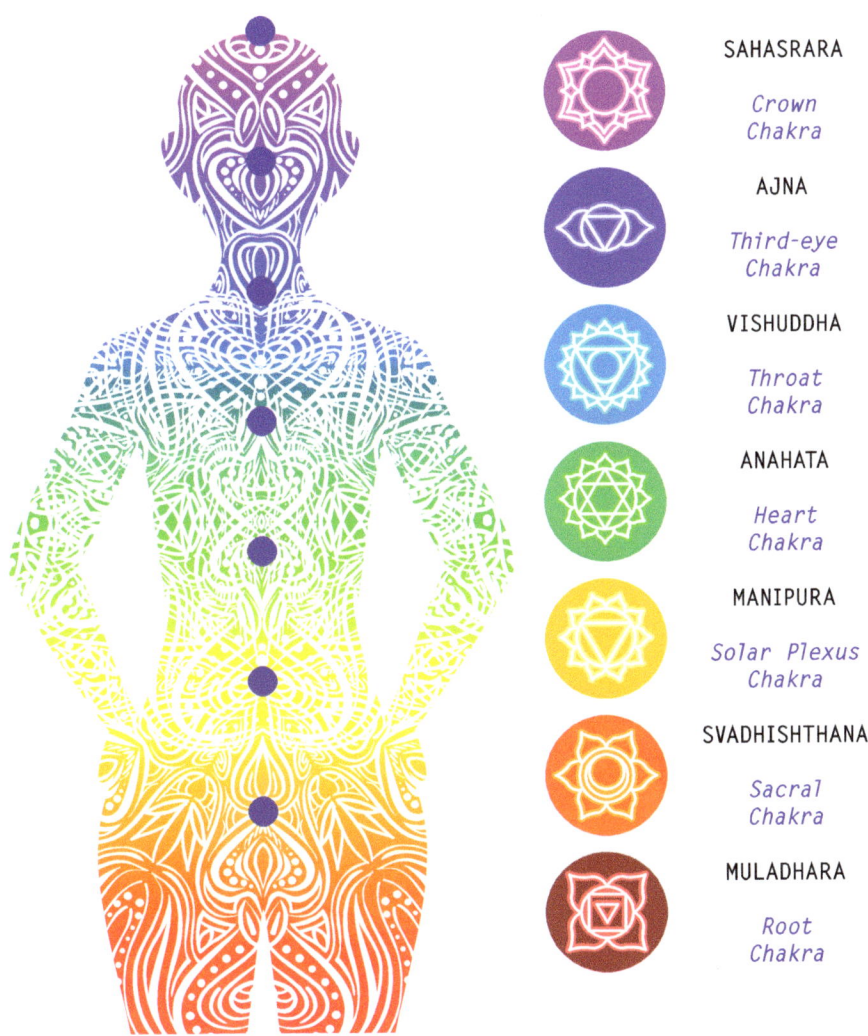

Connection

Balancing the Root Chakra

"Holding on to anger is like grasping a hot coal with the intent of throwing it at someone else — you are the one who gets burned."

– Buddha

- How well do you know yourself? List what makes you feel secure in yourself, your relationships and your external environments.

- What low vibrational emotion is blocking you from experiencing contentment with your body and in your life? Are you holding onto residual anger, inundated with fears, ashamed of your past or overwhelmed with resentment?

- Do you fear you are going to lose your manifestations — your home, professional successes, and relationships? Honestly assess if you live with a sense of security and confidence or fear of losing your abundance.

BALANCE AMONGST THE CHAOS

Date: ____ / ____ / ____

My Daily Intention:

My Affirmation:

What I'm grateful for today:

What I'm doing today:

What the Universe is doing:

Biggest win of the day:

Biggest lesson of the day:

THE DAILY JOURNAL

Date: ___/___/_____

My Daily Intention:

My Affirmation:

What I'm grateful for today:

What I'm doing today:

What the Universe is doing:

Biggest win of the day:

Biggest lesson of the day:

BALANCE AMONGST THE CHAOS

Date: ___ / ___ / ___

My Daily Intention:

My Affirmation:

What I'm grateful for today:

What I'm doing today:

What the Universe is doing:

Biggest win of the day:

Biggest lesson of the day:

THE DAILY JOURNAL

Date: ___ / ___ / ___

My Daily Intention:

My Affirmation:

What I'm grateful for today:

What I'm doing today:

What the Universe is doing:

Biggest win of the day:

Biggest lesson of the day:

BALANCE AMONGST THE CHAOS

Date: ___/___/___

My Daily Intention:

My Affirmation:

What I'm grateful for today:

What I'm doing today:

What the Universe is doing:

Biggest win of the day:

Biggest lesson of the day:

THE DAILY JOURNAL

Date: ___ / ___ / ___

My Daily Intention:

My Affirmation:

What I'm grateful for today:

What I'm doing today:

What the Universe is doing:

Biggest win of the day:

Biggest lesson of the day:

BALANCE AMONGST THE CHAOS

Date: ___/___/___

My Daily Intention:

My Affirmation:

What I'm grateful for today:

What I'm doing today:

What the Universe is doing:

Biggest win of the day:

Biggest lesson of the day:

THE DAILY JOURNAL 41

Date: ___ / ___ / _____

My Daily Intention:

My Affirmation:

What I'm grateful for today:

What I'm doing today:

What the Universe is doing:

Biggest win of the day:

Biggest lesson of the day:

BALANCE AMONGST THE CHAOS

Date: ___/___/___

My Daily Intention:

My Affirmation:

What I'm grateful for today:

What I'm doing today:

What the Universe is doing:

Biggest win of the day:

Biggest lesson of the day:

THE DAILY JOURNAL

Date: ___/___/___

My Daily Intention:

My Affirmation:

What I'm grateful for today:

What I'm doing today:

What the Universe is doing:

Biggest win of the day:

Biggest lesson of the day:

BALANCE AMONGST THE CHAOS

Date: ___/___/___

My Daily Intention:

My Affirmation:

What I'm grateful for today:

What I'm doing today:

What the Universe is doing:

Biggest win of the day:

Biggest lesson of the day:

THE DAILY JOURNAL

Date: ___/___/___

My Daily Intention:

My Affirmation:

What I'm grateful for today:

What I'm doing today:

What the Universe is doing:

Biggest win of the day:

Biggest lesson of the day:

BALANCE AMONGST THE CHAOS

Date: ___ / ___ / ___

My Daily Intention:

My Affirmation:

What I'm grateful for today:

What I'm doing today:

What the Universe is doing:

Biggest win of the day:

Biggest lesson of the day:

THE DAILY JOURNAL   47

Date: ___/___/___

My Daily Intention: My Affirmation:

What I'm grateful for today:

What I'm doing today: What the Universe is doing:

Biggest win of the day:

Biggest lesson of the day:

BALANCE AMONGST THE CHAOS

Date: ___/___/___

My Daily Intention:

My Affirmation:

What I'm grateful for today:

What I'm doing today:

What the Universe is doing:

Biggest win of the day:

Biggest lesson of the day:

THE DAILY JOURNAL

Date: ___ / ___ / ___

My Daily Intention:

My Affirmation:

What I'm grateful for today:

What I'm doing today:

What the Universe is doing:

Biggest win of the day:

Biggest lesson of the day:

BALANCE AMONGST THE CHAOS

Date: ___/___/___

My Daily Intention:

My Affirmation:

What I'm grateful for today:

What I'm doing today:

What the Universe is doing:

Biggest win of the day:

Biggest lesson of the day:

THE DAILY JOURNAL

Date: ___ / ___ / ___

My Daily Intention:

My Affirmation:

What I'm grateful for today:

What I'm doing today:

What the Universe is doing:

Biggest win of the day:

Biggest lesson of the day:

Date: ___ / ___ / ___

My Daily Intention:

My Affirmation:

What I'm grateful for today:

What I'm doing today:

What the Universe is doing:

Biggest win of the day:

Biggest lesson of the day:

THE DAILY JOURNAL

53

Date: ____ / ____ / _____

My Daily Intention:

My Affirmation:

What I'm grateful for today:

What I'm doing today:

What the Universe is doing:

Biggest win of the day:

Biggest lesson of the day:

BALANCE AMONGST THE CHAOS

Date: ___/___/___

My Daily Intention:

My Affirmation:

What I'm grateful for today:

What I'm doing today:

What the Universe is doing:

Biggest win of the day:

Biggest lesson of the day:

THE DAILY JOURNAL

Date: ___/___/___

My Daily Intention:

My Affirmation:

What I'm grateful for today:

What I'm doing today:

What the Universe is doing:

Biggest win of the day:

Biggest lesson of the day:

Date: ___ / ___ / ___

My Daily Intention:

My Affirmation:

What I'm grateful for today:

What I'm doing today:

What the Universe is doing:

Biggest win of the day:

Biggest lesson of the day:

THE DAILY JOURNAL

Date: ___ / ___ / ___

My Daily Intention:

My Affirmation:

What I'm grateful for today:

What I'm doing today:

What the Universe is doing:

Biggest win of the day:

Biggest lesson of the day:

Date: ___ / ___ / ___

My Daily Intention:

My Affirmation:

What I'm grateful for today:

What I'm doing today:

What the Universe is doing:

Biggest win of the day:

Biggest lesson of the day:

THE DAILY JOURNAL 59

Date: ___ / ___ / ___

My Daily Intention:

My Affirmation:

What I'm grateful for today:

What I'm doing today:

What the Universe is doing:

Biggest win of the day:

Biggest lesson of the day:

Date: ___/___/___

My Daily Intention:

My Affirmation:

What I'm grateful for today:

What I'm doing today:

What the Universe is doing:

Biggest win of the day:

Biggest lesson of the day:

THE DAILY JOURNAL

Date: ____ / ____ / ____

My Daily Intention:

My Affirmation:

What I'm grateful for today:

What I'm doing today:

What the Universe is doing:

Biggest win of the day:

Biggest lesson of the day:

BALANCE AMONGST THE CHAOS

Date: ___ / ___ / ___

My Daily Intention:

My Affirmation:

What I'm grateful for today:

What I'm doing today:

What the Universe is doing:

Biggest win of the day:

Biggest lesson of the day:

THE DAILY JOURNAL

Date: ___ / ___ / ___

My Daily Intention:

My Affirmation:

What I'm grateful for today:

What I'm doing today:

What the Universe is doing:

Biggest win of the day:

Biggest lesson of the day:

Patience

Balancing the Sacral Chakra

"Everything good takes time. Don't do work in a hurry. Go into details; it pays in every way. Time means power for your work. Mediocrity is always in a rush; but whatever is worth doing at all is worth doing with consideration. For genius is nothing more nor less than doing well what anyone can do badly."

- Amelia Barr, 9 Rules for Success

❖ Patience is also a form of action. Do you find yourself often impatient with others if they do not perform or behave to your liking?

- Being in a hurry to improve yourself only slows down the process. Are you rushing through your days? Do you take a moment to enjoy how your meal tastes, are you present during your workouts and do you enjoy your friends' company? List the emotions, situations or people that make you feel rushed and the moments when you feel relaxed and at ease.

- Are you in a toxic cycle of restricting and bingeing? Do you limit yourself from enjoying pleasure and then splurge to the point of imbalance? Reflect on your relationship with experiencing pleasure.

BALANCE AMONGST THE CHAOS

Date: ___/___/___

My Daily Intention:

My Affirmation:

What I'm grateful for today:

What I'm doing today:

What the Universe is doing:

Biggest win of the day:

Biggest lesson of the day:

THE DAILY JOURNAL

Date: ___ / ___ / ___

My Daily Intention:

My Affirmation:

What I'm grateful for today:

What I'm doing today:

What the Universe is doing:

Biggest win of the day:

Biggest lesson of the day:

Date: ___/___/___

My Daily Intention:

My Affirmation:

What I'm grateful for today:

What I'm doing today:

What the Universe is doing:

Biggest win of the day:

Biggest lesson of the day:

THE DAILY JOURNAL

Date: ____ / ____ / ____

My Daily Intention:

My Affirmation:

What I'm grateful for today:

What I'm doing today:

What the Universe is doing:

Biggest win of the day:

Biggest lesson of the day:

BALANCE AMONGST THE CHAOS

Date: ___ / ___ / ___

My Daily Intention:

My Affirmation:

What I'm grateful for today:

What I'm doing today:

What the Universe is doing:

Biggest win of the day:

Biggest lesson of the day:

THE DAILY JOURNAL

Date: ___ / ___ / ___

My Daily Intention:

My Affirmation:

What I'm grateful for today:

What I'm doing today:

What the Universe is doing:

Biggest win of the day:

Biggest lesson of the day:

Date: / /

My Daily Intention:

My Affirmation:

What I'm grateful for today:

What I'm doing today:

What the Universe is doing:

Biggest win of the day:

Biggest lesson of the day:

THE DAILY JOURNAL

Date: ___ / ___ / ___

My Daily Intention:

My Affirmation:

What I'm grateful for today:

What I'm doing today:

What the Universe is doing:

Biggest win of the day:

Biggest lesson of the day:

BALANCE AMONGST THE CHAOS

Date: ___ / ___ / ___

My Daily Intention:

My Affirmation:

What I'm grateful for today:

What I'm doing today:

What the Universe is doing:

Biggest win of the day:

Biggest lesson of the day:

THE DAILY JOURNAL

Date: ___ / ___ / ___

My Daily Intention:

My Affirmation:

What I'm grateful for today:

What I'm doing today:

What the Universe is doing:

Biggest win of the day:

Biggest lesson of the day:

BALANCE AMONGST THE CHAOS

Date: ___ / ___ / ___

My Daily Intention:

My Affirmation:

What I'm grateful for today:

What I'm doing today:

What the Universe is doing:

Biggest win of the day:

Biggest lesson of the day:

THE DAILY JOURNAL

Date: ___ / ___ / ___

My Daily Intention:

My Affirmation:

What I'm grateful for today:

What I'm doing today:

What the Universe is doing:

Biggest win of the day:

Biggest lesson of the day:

Date: ___ / ___ / ___

My Daily Intention:

My Affirmation:

What I'm grateful for today:

What I'm doing today:

What the Universe is doing:

Biggest win of the day:

Biggest lesson of the day:

THE DAILY JOURNAL

Date: ___/___/___

My Daily Intention:

My Affirmation:

What I'm grateful for today:

What I'm doing today:

What the Universe is doing:

Biggest win of the day:

Biggest lesson of the day:

BALANCE AMONGST THE CHAOS

Date: ___ / ___ / _____

My Daily Intention:

My Affirmation:

What I'm grateful for today:

What I'm doing today:

What the Universe is doing:

Biggest win of the day:

Biggest lesson of the day:

THE DAILY JOURNAL

Date: ___ / ___ / ___

My Daily Intention:

My Affirmation:

What I'm grateful for today:

What I'm doing today:

What the Universe is doing:

Biggest win of the day:

Biggest lesson of the day:

BALANCE AMONGST THE CHAOS

Date: ___/___/___

My Daily Intention:

My Affirmation:

What I'm grateful for today:

What I'm doing today:

What the Universe is doing:

Biggest win of the day:

Biggest lesson of the day:

THE DAILY JOURNAL

Date: ___ / ___ / ___

My Daily Intention:

My Affirmation:

What I'm grateful for today:

What I'm doing today:

What the Universe is doing:

Biggest win of the day:

Biggest lesson of the day:

BALANCE AMONGST THE CHAOS

Date: ___/___/___

My Daily Intention:

My Affirmation:

What I'm grateful for today:

What I'm doing today:

What the Universe is doing:

Biggest win of the day:

Biggest lesson of the day:

THE DAILY JOURNAL

Date: ___ / ___ / ___

My Daily Intention:

My Affirmation:

What I'm grateful for today:

What I'm doing today:

What the Universe is doing:

Biggest win of the day:

Biggest lesson of the day:

Date: ___/___/___

My Daily Intention:

My Affirmation:

What I'm grateful for today:

What I'm doing today:

What the Universe is doing:

Biggest win of the day:

Biggest lesson of the day:

THE DAILY JOURNAL

Date: ____ / ____ / ____

My Daily Intention:

My Affirmation:

What I'm grateful for today:

What I'm doing today:

What the Universe is doing:

Biggest win of the day:

Biggest lesson of the day:

BALANCE AMONGST THE CHAOS

Date: ___ / ___ / ___

My Daily Intention:

My Affirmation:

What I'm grateful for today:

What I'm doing today:

What the Universe is doing:

Biggest win of the day:

Biggest lesson of the day:

THE DAILY JOURNAL

Date: ___ / ___ / ___

My Daily Intention:

My Affirmation:

What I'm grateful for today:

What I'm doing today:

What the Universe is doing:

Biggest win of the day:

Biggest lesson of the day:

BALANCE AMONGST THE CHAOS

Date: ___/___/___

My Daily Intention:

My Affirmation:

What I'm grateful for today:

What I'm doing today:

What the Universe is doing:

Biggest win of the day:

Biggest lesson of the day:

THE DAILY JOURNAL

Date: ___ / ___ / ___

My Daily Intention:

My Affirmation:

What I'm grateful for today:

What I'm doing today:

What the Universe is doing:

Biggest win of the day:

Biggest lesson of the day:

BALANCE AMONGST THE CHAOS

Date: ___ / ___ / ___

My Daily Intention:

My Affirmation:

What I'm grateful for today:

What I'm doing today:

What the Universe is doing:

Biggest win of the day:

Biggest lesson of the day:

THE DAILY JOURNAL

Date: ___ / ___ / ___

My Daily Intention:

My Affirmation:

What I'm grateful for today:

What I'm doing today:

What the Universe is doing:

Biggest win of the day:

Biggest lesson of the day:

Date: ___/___/___

My Daily Intention:

My Affirmation:

What I'm grateful for today:

What I'm doing today:

What the Universe is doing:

Biggest win of the day:

Biggest lesson of the day:

THE DAILY JOURNAL

Date: ___ / ___ / ___

My Daily Intention:

My Affirmation:

What I'm grateful for today:

What I'm doing today:

What the Universe is doing:

Biggest win of the day:

Biggest lesson of the day:

Confidence

Balancing the Solar Plexus Chakra

"With realization of one's own potential and self-confidence in one's ability, one can build a better world."

- Dalai Lama

- Do you apologize before or after saying something you have every intention of stating? How often do you say sorry for speaking or living your truth? Reflect on what you are sorry for — it is probably a very short list.

- When making any life decision, do you require the opinion of two or more people before you declare your decision? Reflect on two people you routinely seek personal or professional advice from. List these people's positive qualities and remind yourself why these two specific opinions satisfy your needs.

✸ Is your confidence embedded in the validation of others? Evaluate what makes you feel worthy of success or love.

Date: ___ / ___ / ___

My Daily Intention:

My Affirmation:

What I'm grateful for today:

What I'm doing today:

What the Universe is doing:

Biggest win of the day:

Biggest lesson of the day:

THE DAILY JOURNAL

Date: ____ / ____ / ____

My Daily Intention:

My Affirmation:

What I'm grateful for today:

What I'm doing today:

What the Universe is doing:

Biggest win of the day:

Biggest lesson of the day:

BALANCE AMONGST THE CHAOS

Date: ____/____/____

My Daily Intention:

My Affirmation:

What I'm grateful for today:

What I'm doing today:

What the Universe is doing:

Biggest win of the day:

Biggest lesson of the day:

THE DAILY JOURNAL

Date: ____ / ____ / _____

My Daily Intention:

My Affirmation:

What I'm grateful for today:

What I'm doing today:

What the Universe is doing:

Biggest win of the day:

Biggest lesson of the day:

BALANCE AMONGST THE CHAOS

Date: ____ / ____ / ____

My Daily Intention:

My Affirmation:

What I'm grateful for today:

What I'm doing today:

What the Universe is doing:

Biggest win of the day:

Biggest lesson of the day:

THE DAILY JOURNAL

Date: ___ / ___ / ___

My Daily Intention:

My Affirmation:

What I'm grateful for today:

What I'm doing today:

What the Universe is doing:

Biggest win of the day:

Biggest lesson of the day:

Date: ___ / ___ / ___

My Daily Intention:

My Affirmation:

What I'm grateful for today:

What I'm doing today:

What the Universe is doing:

Biggest win of the day:

Biggest lesson of the day:

THE DAILY JOURNAL

Date: ____ / ____ / ____

My Daily Intention:

My Affirmation:

What I'm grateful for today:

What I'm doing today:

What the Universe is doing:

Biggest win of the day:

Biggest lesson of the day:

Date: ___/___/___

My Daily Intention:

My Affirmation:

What I'm grateful for today:

What I'm doing today:

What the Universe is doing:

Biggest win of the day:

Biggest lesson of the day:

THE DAILY JOURNAL

Date: ____ / ____ / ____

My Daily Intention:

My Affirmation:

What I'm grateful for today:

What I'm doing today:

What the Universe is doing:

Biggest win of the day:

Biggest lesson of the day:

Date: ___/___/___

My Daily Intention:

My Affirmation:

What I'm grateful for today:

What I'm doing today:

What the Universe is doing:

Biggest win of the day:

Biggest lesson of the day:

THE DAILY JOURNAL

Date: ____ / ____ / ____

My Daily Intention:

My Affirmation:

What I'm grateful for today:

What I'm doing today:

What the Universe is doing:

Biggest win of the day:

Biggest lesson of the day:

Date: ____/____/____

My Daily Intention:

My Affirmation:

What I'm grateful for today:

What I'm doing today:

What the Universe is doing:

Biggest win of the day:

Biggest lesson of the day:

THE DAILY JOURNAL

Date: ____ / ____ / ____

My Daily Intention:

My Affirmation:

What I'm grateful for today:

What I'm doing today:

What the Universe is doing:

Biggest win of the day:

Biggest lesson of the day:

Date: /   /

My Daily Intention:

My Affirmation:

What I'm grateful for today:

What I'm doing today:

What the Universe is doing:

Biggest win of the day:

Biggest lesson of the day:

THE DAILY JOURNAL

Date: ___ / ___ / ___

My Daily Intention:

My Affirmation:

What I'm grateful for today:

What I'm doing today:

What the Universe is doing:

Biggest win of the day:

Biggest lesson of the day:

BALANCE AMONGST THE CHAOS

Date: ___ / ___ / ___

My Daily Intention:

My Affirmation:

What I'm grateful for today:

What I'm doing today:

What the Universe is doing:

Biggest win of the day:

Biggest lesson of the day:

THE DAILY JOURNAL

Date: ____ / ____ / ____

My Daily Intention:

My Affirmation:

What I'm grateful for today:

What I'm doing today:

What the Universe is doing:

Biggest win of the day:

Biggest lesson of the day:

Date: ___ / ___ / ___

My Daily Intention:

My Affirmation:

What I'm grateful for today:

What I'm doing today:

What the Universe is doing:

Biggest win of the day:

Biggest lesson of the day:

THE DAILY JOURNAL

Date: ____ / ____ / ____

My Daily Intention:

My Affirmation:

What I'm grateful for today:

What I'm doing today:

What the Universe is doing:

Biggest win of the day:

Biggest lesson of the day:

Date: ___ / ___ / ___

My Daily Intention:

My Affirmation:

What I'm grateful for today:

What I'm doing today:

What the Universe is doing:

Biggest win of the day:

Biggest lesson of the day:

THE DAILY JOURNAL

Date: ___ / ___ / ___

My Daily Intention:

My Affirmation:

What I'm grateful for today:

What I'm doing today:

What the Universe is doing:

Biggest win of the day:

Biggest lesson of the day:

Date: ___/___/___

My Daily Intention:

My Affirmation:

What I'm grateful for today:

What I'm doing today:

What the Universe is doing:

Biggest win of the day:

Biggest lesson of the day:

THE DAILY JOURNAL

Date: ____ / ____ / ____

My Daily Intention:

My Affirmation:

What I'm grateful for today:

What I'm doing today:

What the Universe is doing:

Biggest win of the day:

Biggest lesson of the day:

Date: ___/___/___

My Daily Intention:

My Affirmation:

What I'm grateful for today:

What I'm doing today:

What the Universe is doing:

Biggest win of the day:

Biggest lesson of the day:

THE DAILY JOURNAL

Date: ___ / ___ / _____

My Daily Intention:

My Affirmation:

What I'm grateful for today:

What I'm doing today:

What the Universe is doing:

Biggest win of the day:

Biggest lesson of the day:

Date: ___ / ___ / ___

My Daily Intention:

My Affirmation:

What I'm grateful for today:

What I'm doing today:

What the Universe is doing:

Biggest win of the day:

Biggest lesson of the day:

THE DAILY JOURNAL

Date: ___ / ___ / ___

My Daily Intention:

My Affirmation:

What I'm grateful for today:

What I'm doing today:

What the Universe is doing:

Biggest win of the day:

Biggest lesson of the day:

Date: ___ / ___ / ___

My Daily Intention:

My Affirmation:

What I'm grateful for today:

What I'm doing today:

What the Universe is doing:

Biggest win of the day:

Biggest lesson of the day:

THE DAILY JOURNAL

Date: ____ / ____ / ____

My Daily Intention:

My Affirmation:

What I'm grateful for today:

What I'm doing today:

What the Universe is doing:

Biggest win of the day:

Biggest lesson of the day:

Gratitude

Balancing the Heart Chakra

"To forgive is to set a prisoner free and discover that prisoner was you."

- Lewis B. Smedes

- Is there any grief blocking your heart? Is there a previous relationship, loss of a loved one, or pain from a past situation still weighing on your heart? Process your thoughts here by drawing a mind map:

✻ Do you need to forgive anyone else for past mistakes? List who has hurt you and what they have done. Write a letter offering forgiveness to this person:

- Do you need to forgive yourself for any past mistakes? Reflect on a time you may have sabotaged yourself or failed to live up to your own expectations. Write an apology letter to yourself:

- Are you able to show yourself unconditional love and compassion? Do you struggle to accept love from others? List the reasons why you are worthy of love and acceptance:

THE DAILY JOURNAL

Date: ___ / ___ / ___

My Daily Intention:

My Affirmation:

What I'm grateful for today:

What I'm doing today:

What the Universe is doing:

Biggest win of the day:

Biggest lesson of the day:

BALANCE AMONGST THE CHAOS

Date: ___/___/_____

My Daily Intention:

My Affirmation:

What I'm grateful for today:

What I'm doing today:

What the Universe is doing:

Biggest win of the day:

Biggest lesson of the day:

THE DAILY JOURNAL

Date: ____ / ____ / ____

My Daily Intention:
_____
_____
_____

My Affirmation:
_____
_____
_____

What I'm grateful for today:
_____
_____
_____

What I'm doing today:
_____
_____
_____
_____
_____

What the Universe is doing:
_____
_____
_____
_____
_____

Biggest win of the day:
_____
_____

Biggest lesson of the day:
_____
_____

BALANCE AMONGST THE CHAOS

Date: ___/___/___

My Daily Intention:

My Affirmation:

What I'm grateful for today:

What I'm doing today:

What the Universe is doing:

Biggest win of the day:

Biggest lesson of the day:

THE DAILY JOURNAL

Date: ____ / ____ / _____

My Daily Intention:
_____
_____
_____

My Affirmation:
_____
_____
_____

What I'm grateful for today:
_____
_____
_____

What I'm doing today:
_____
_____
_____
_____
_____
_____

What the Universe is doing:
_____
_____
_____
_____
_____
_____

Biggest win of the day:
_____
_____
_____

Biggest lesson of the day:
_____
_____
_____

Date: ___/___/___

My Daily Intention:

My Affirmation:

What I'm grateful for today:

What I'm doing today:

What the Universe is doing:

Biggest win of the day:

Biggest lesson of the day:

THE DAILY JOURNAL

Date: ___ / ___ / ___

My Daily Intention:

My Affirmation:

What I'm grateful for today:

What I'm doing today:

What the Universe is doing:

Biggest win of the day:

Biggest lesson of the day:

BALANCE AMONGST THE CHAOS

Date: ___/___/___

My Daily Intention:
_____
_____

My Affirmation:
_____
_____

What I'm grateful for today:
_____
_____

What I'm doing today:
_____
_____
_____
_____
_____

What the Universe is doing:
_____
_____
_____
_____
_____

Biggest win of the day:
_____
_____

Biggest lesson of the day:
_____
_____

THE DAILY JOURNAL

Date: ___ / ___ / ___

My Daily Intention:

My Affirmation:

What I'm grateful for today:

What I'm doing today:

What the Universe is doing:

Biggest win of the day:

Biggest lesson of the day:

Date: ___/___/_____

My Daily Intention:

My Affirmation:

What I'm grateful for today:

What I'm doing today:

What the Universe is doing:

Biggest win of the day:

Biggest lesson of the day:

THE DAILY JOURNAL

Date: ___ / ___ / ___

My Daily Intention:

My Affirmation:

What I'm grateful for today:

What I'm doing today:

What the Universe is doing:

Biggest win of the day:

Biggest lesson of the day:

Date: ___ / ___ / ___

My Daily Intention:

My Affirmation:

What I'm grateful for today:

What I'm doing today:

What the Universe is doing:

Biggest win of the day:

Biggest lesson of the day:

THE DAILY JOURNAL

Date: ___ / ___ / ___

My Daily Intention:

My Affirmation:

What I'm grateful for today:

What I'm doing today:

What the Universe is doing:

Biggest win of the day:

Biggest lesson of the day:

Date: ___/___/___

My Daily Intention:

My Affirmation:

What I'm grateful for today:

What I'm doing today:

What the Universe is doing:

Biggest win of the day:

Biggest lesson of the day:

THE DAILY JOURNAL

Date: ___ / ___ / ___

My Daily Intention:

My Affirmation:

What I'm grateful for today:

What I'm doing today:

What the Universe is doing:

Biggest win of the day:

Biggest lesson of the day:

BALANCE AMONGST THE CHAOS

Date: ___ / ___ / _____

My Daily Intention:

My Affirmation:

What I'm grateful for today:

What I'm doing today:

What the Universe is doing:

Biggest win of the day:

Biggest lesson of the day:

THE DAILY JOURNAL

Date: ___ / ___ / ___

My Daily Intention:
_____
_____
_____

My Affirmation:
_____
_____
_____

What I'm grateful for today:
_____
_____
_____

What I'm doing today:
_____
_____
_____
_____
_____
_____

What the Universe is doing:
_____
_____
_____
_____
_____
_____

Biggest win of the day:
_____
_____
_____

Biggest lesson of the day:
_____
_____
_____

Date: ___ / ___ / ___

My Daily Intention:

My Affirmation:

What I'm grateful for today:

What I'm doing today:

What the Universe is doing:

Biggest win of the day:

Biggest lesson of the day:

THE DAILY JOURNAL

Date: _____ / _____ / _____

My Daily Intention:

My Affirmation:

What I'm grateful for today:

What I'm doing today:

What the Universe is doing:

Biggest win of the day:

Biggest lesson of the day:

Date: ___/___/___

My Daily Intention:

My Affirmation:

What I'm grateful for today:

What I'm doing today:

What the Universe is doing:

Biggest win of the day:

Biggest lesson of the day:

THE DAILY JOURNAL

Date: _____ / _____ / _____

My Daily Intention:

My Affirmation:

What I'm grateful for today:

What I'm doing today:

What the Universe is doing:

Biggest win of the day:

Biggest lesson of the day:

BALANCE AMONGST THE CHAOS

Date: ___ / ___ / ___

My Daily Intention:

My Affirmation:

What I'm grateful for today:

What I'm doing today:

What the Universe is doing:

Biggest win of the day:

Biggest lesson of the day:

THE DAILY JOURNAL

Date: ___ / ___ / ___

My Daily Intention:

My Affirmation:

What I'm grateful for today:

What I'm doing today:

What the Universe is doing:

Biggest win of the day:

Biggest lesson of the day:

Date: ___/___/___

My Daily Intention:

My Affirmation:

What I'm grateful for today:

What I'm doing today:

What the Universe is doing:

Biggest win of the day:

Biggest lesson of the day:

THE DAILY JOURNAL

Date: ___ / ___ / ___

My Daily Intention:

My Affirmation:

What I'm grateful for today:

What I'm doing today:

What the Universe is doing:

Biggest win of the day:

Biggest lesson of the day:

Date: ___/___/___

My Daily Intention:

My Affirmation:

What I'm grateful for today:

What I'm doing today:

What the Universe is doing:

Biggest win of the day:

Biggest lesson of the day:

THE DAILY JOURNAL

Date: ____ / ____ / ____

My Daily Intention:

My Affirmation:

What I'm grateful for today:

What I'm doing today:

What the Universe is doing:

Biggest win of the day:

Biggest lesson of the day:

BALANCE AMONGST THE CHAOS

Date: ___ / ___ / ___

My Daily Intention:

My Affirmation:

What I'm grateful for today:

What I'm doing today:

What the Universe is doing:

Biggest win of the day:

Biggest lesson of the day:

THE DAILY JOURNAL

Date: ____ / ____ / ____

My Daily Intention:

My Affirmation:

What I'm grateful for today:

What I'm doing today:

What the Universe is doing:

Biggest win of the day:

Biggest lesson of the day:

Solitude

Balancing the Throat Chakra

"Our true home is what Buddha called the island of self, the peaceful place inside of us. Oftentimes, we don't notice it's there; we don't even really know where we are, because our outer and inner environment is filled with noise. We need some quietness to find that island of self."

- Thich Nhat Hanh

- Do you struggle to spend time by yourself or do you appreciate it? List your favorite things to do in your free time, away from social media and socializing:

❖ Do you find yourself responding to others without actually listening to them first? Reflect on a friend or colleague who is a phenomenal listener. How do they make you feel and what positive attributes do you wish to adopt for yourself? Explain here:

❖ Has there been a time you felt compromised using your voice for fear of being judged or shamed for your opinion? Make a list and evaluate the emotions restraining your opinion:

BALANCE AMONGST THE CHAOS

Date: ___ / ___ / _____

My Daily Intention:

My Affirmation:

What I'm grateful for today:

What I'm doing today:

What the Universe is doing:

Biggest win of the day:

Biggest lesson of the day:

THE DAILY JOURNAL

Date: ____ / ____ / _____

My Daily Intention:

My Affirmation:

What I'm grateful for today:

What I'm doing today:

What the Universe is doing:

Biggest win of the day:

Biggest lesson of the day:

BALANCE AMONGST THE CHAOS

Date: ___ / ___ / ___

My Daily Intention:

My Affirmation:

What I'm grateful for today:

What I'm doing today:

What the Universe is doing:

Biggest win of the day:

Biggest lesson of the day:

THE DAILY JOURNAL

Date: ___ / ___ / ___

My Daily Intention:

My Affirmation:

What I'm grateful for today:

What I'm doing today:

What the Universe is doing:

Biggest win of the day:

Biggest lesson of the day:

BALANCE AMONGST THE CHAOS

Date: /   /

My Daily Intention:

My Affirmation:

What I'm grateful for today:

What I'm doing today:

What the Universe is doing:

Biggest win of the day:

Biggest lesson of the day:

THE DAILY JOURNAL

Date: ___ / ___ / ___

My Daily Intention:

My Affirmation:

What I'm grateful for today:

What I'm doing today:

What the Universe is doing:

Biggest win of the day:

Biggest lesson of the day:

BALANCE AMONGST THE CHAOS

Date: /   /

My Daily Intention:

My Affirmation:

What I'm grateful for today:

What I'm doing today:

What the Universe is doing:

Biggest win of the day:

Biggest lesson of the day:

THE DAILY JOURNAL

Date: _____ / _____ / _____

My Daily Intention:

My Affirmation:

What I'm grateful for today:

What I'm doing today:

What the Universe is doing:

Biggest win of the day:

Biggest lesson of the day:

BALANCE AMONGST THE CHAOS

Date: ___ / ___ / ___

My Daily Intention:

My Affirmation:

What I'm grateful for today:

What I'm doing today:

What the Universe is doing:

Biggest win of the day:

Biggest lesson of the day:

THE DAILY JOURNAL

Date: ____ / ____ / ____

My Daily Intention:

My Affirmation:

What I'm grateful for today:

What I'm doing today:

What the Universe is doing:

Biggest win of the day:

Biggest lesson of the day:

BALANCE AMONGST THE CHAOS

Date: ___/___/___

My Daily Intention:

My Affirmation:

What I'm grateful for today:

What I'm doing today:

What the Universe is doing:

Biggest win of the day:

Biggest lesson of the day:

THE DAILY JOURNAL

Date: ___ / ___ / ___

My Daily Intention:

My Affirmation:

What I'm grateful for today:

What I'm doing today:

What the Universe is doing:

Biggest win of the day:

Biggest lesson of the day:

BALANCE AMONGST THE CHAOS

Date: ___ / ___ / _____

My Daily Intention:

My Affirmation:

What I'm grateful for today:

What I'm doing today:

What the Universe is doing:

Biggest win of the day:

Biggest lesson of the day:

THE DAILY JOURNAL

Date: ___ / ___ / ___

My Daily Intention:

My Affirmation:

What I'm grateful for today:

What I'm doing today:

What the Universe is doing:

Biggest win of the day:

Biggest lesson of the day:

BALANCE AMONGST THE CHAOS

Date: /   /

My Daily Intention:

My Affirmation:

What I'm grateful for today:

What I'm doing today:

What the Universe is doing:

Biggest win of the day:

Biggest lesson of the day:

THE DAILY JOURNAL

Date: ___ / ___ / ___

My Daily Intention:

My Affirmation:

What I'm grateful for today:

What I'm doing today:

What the Universe is doing:

Biggest win of the day:

Biggest lesson of the day:

BALANCE AMONGST THE CHAOS

Date: ___ / ___ / _____

My Daily Intention:

My Affirmation:

What I'm grateful for today:

What I'm doing today:

What the Universe is doing:

Biggest win of the day:

Biggest lesson of the day:

THE DAILY JOURNAL

Date: ___ / ___ / ___

My Daily Intention:

My Affirmation:

What I'm grateful for today:

What I'm doing today:

What the Universe is doing:

Biggest win of the day:

Biggest lesson of the day:

Date: /   /

My Daily Intention:

My Affirmation:

What I'm grateful for today:

What I'm doing today:

What the Universe is doing:

Biggest win of the day:

Biggest lesson of the day:

THE DAILY JOURNAL

Date: ___ / ___ / ___

My Daily Intention:

My Affirmation:

What I'm grateful for today:

What I'm doing today:

What the Universe is doing:

Biggest win of the day:

Biggest lesson of the day:

BALANCE AMONGST THE CHAOS

Date: /   /

My Daily Intention:

My Affirmation:

What I'm grateful for today:

What I'm doing today:

What the Universe is doing:

Biggest win of the day:

Biggest lesson of the day:

THE DAILY JOURNAL

Date: ___ / ___ / ___

My Daily Intention:

My Affirmation:

What I'm grateful for today:

What I'm doing today:

What the Universe is doing:

Biggest win of the day:

Biggest lesson of the day:

BALANCE AMONGST THE CHAOS

Date: ___ / ___ / ___

My Daily Intention:

My Affirmation:

What I'm grateful for today:

What I'm doing today:

What the Universe is doing:

Biggest win of the day:

Biggest lesson of the day:

THE DAILY JOURNAL

Date: ___ / ___ / ___

My Daily Intention:

My Affirmation:

What I'm grateful for today:

What I'm doing today:

What the Universe is doing:

Biggest win of the day:

Biggest lesson of the day:

BALANCE AMONGST THE CHAOS

Date: ___/___/___

My Daily Intention:

My Affirmation:

What I'm grateful for today:

What I'm doing today:

What the Universe is doing:

Biggest win of the day:

Biggest lesson of the day:

THE DAILY JOURNAL

Date: ____ / ____ / ____

My Daily Intention:

My Affirmation:

What I'm grateful for today:

What I'm doing today:

What the Universe is doing:

Biggest win of the day:

Biggest lesson of the day:

BALANCE AMONGST THE CHAOS

Date: ___/___/___

My Daily Intention:
_____
_____
_____

My Affirmation:
_____
_____
_____

What I'm grateful for today:
_____
_____
_____

What I'm doing today:
_____
_____
_____
_____
_____
_____
_____

What the Universe is doing:
_____
_____
_____
_____
_____
_____
_____

Biggest win of the day:
_____
_____
_____

Biggest lesson of the day:
_____
_____
_____

THE DAILY JOURNAL

Date: ___ / ___ / ___

My Daily Intention:

My Affirmation:

What I'm grateful for today:

What I'm doing today:

What the Universe is doing:

Biggest win of the day:

Biggest lesson of the day:

BALANCE AMONGST THE CHAOS

Date: ___ / ___ / ___

My Daily Intention:

My Affirmation:

What I'm grateful for today:

What I'm doing today:

What the Universe is doing:

Biggest win of the day:

Biggest lesson of the day:

THE DAILY JOURNAL

Date: ____ / ____ / ____

My Daily Intention:

My Affirmation:

What I'm grateful for today:

What I'm doing today:

What the Universe is doing:

Biggest win of the day:

Biggest lesson of the day:

Intuition

Balancing the Third Eye Chakra

"Your time is limited, so don't waste it living someone else's life. Don't be trapped by dogma, which is living the result of other people's thinking. Don't let the noise of other opinions drown your own inner voice. And most important, have the courage to follow your heart and intuition, they somehow already know what you truly want to become. Everything else is secondary."

- Steve Jobs

- Can you reflect on a specific time when you chose to ignore your intuition? What emotion was blocking you from listening to your gut?

- Do you consider yourself a freethinker? What does it mean for you to be awake?

THE DAILY JOURNAL

❁ Do you trust yourself? Reflect on a situation when you undoubtedly trusted your intuition and something good came of it. Write about that situation here:

BALANCE AMONGST THE CHAOS

Date: ___/___/___

My Daily Intention:

My Affirmation:

What I'm grateful for today:

What I'm doing today:

What the Universe is doing:

Biggest win of the day:

Biggest lesson of the day:

THE DAILY JOURNAL

Date: ____ / ____ / _____

My Daily Intention:
_____
_____
_____

My Affirmation:
_____
_____
_____

What I'm grateful for today:
_____
_____
_____

What I'm doing today:
_____
_____
_____
_____
_____
_____
_____

What the Universe is doing:
_____
_____
_____
_____
_____
_____
_____

Biggest win of the day:
_____
_____
_____

Biggest lesson of the day:
_____
_____
_____

Date: ____ / ____ / ____

My Daily Intention:

My Affirmation:

What I'm grateful for today:

What I'm doing today:

What the Universe is doing:

Biggest win of the day:

Biggest lesson of the day:

THE DAILY JOURNAL

Date: _____ / _____ / _____

My Daily Intention:

My Affirmation:

What I'm grateful for today:

What I'm doing today:

What the Universe is doing:

Biggest win of the day:

Biggest lesson of the day:

Date: ____ / ____ / _____

My Daily Intention:

My Affirmation:

What I'm grateful for today:

What I'm doing today:

What the Universe is doing:

Biggest win of the day:

Biggest lesson of the day:

THE DAILY JOURNAL

Date: ____ / ____ / ____

My Daily Intention:
_____
_____
_____

My Affirmation:
_____
_____
_____

What I'm grateful for today:
_____
_____
_____

What I'm doing today:
_____
_____
_____
_____
_____
_____

What the Universe is doing:
_____
_____
_____
_____
_____
_____

Biggest win of the day:
_____
_____
_____

Biggest lesson of the day:
_____
_____
_____

Date: ____ / ____ / ____

My Daily Intention:

My Affirmation:

What I'm grateful for today:

What I'm doing today:

What the Universe is doing:

Biggest win of the day:

Biggest lesson of the day:

THE DAILY JOURNAL

Date: ____ / ____ / ____

My Daily Intention:
_____
_____

My Affirmation:
_____
_____

What I'm grateful for today:
_____
_____
_____

What I'm doing today:
_____
_____
_____
_____
_____
_____

What the Universe is doing:
_____
_____
_____
_____
_____
_____

Biggest win of the day:
_____
_____
_____

Biggest lesson of the day:
_____
_____
_____

BALANCE AMONGST THE CHAOS

Date: ___ / ___ / ___

My Daily Intention:

My Affirmation:

What I'm grateful for today:

What I'm doing today:

What the Universe is doing:

Biggest win of the day:

Biggest lesson of the day:

THE DAILY JOURNAL

Date: ___ / ___ / ___

My Daily Intention:

My Affirmation:

What I'm grateful for today:

What I'm doing today:

What the Universe is doing:

Biggest win of the day:

Biggest lesson of the day:

Date: ___ / ___ / ___

My Daily Intention:

My Affirmation:

What I'm grateful for today:

What I'm doing today:

What the Universe is doing:

Biggest win of the day:

Biggest lesson of the day:

THE DAILY JOURNAL

Date: _____ / _____ / _____

My Daily Intention:
_____
_____
_____

My Affirmation:
_____
_____
_____

What I'm grateful for today:
_____
_____
_____

What I'm doing today:
_____
_____
_____
_____
_____
_____
_____

What the Universe is doing:
_____
_____
_____
_____
_____
_____
_____

Biggest win of the day:
_____
_____
_____

Biggest lesson of the day:
_____
_____
_____

Date: ___ / ___ / ___

My Daily Intention:

My Affirmation:

What I'm grateful for today:

What I'm doing today:

What the Universe is doing:

Biggest win of the day:

Biggest lesson of the day:

THE DAILY JOURNAL

Date: ___ / ___ / ___

My Daily Intention:
_____
_____
_____

My Affirmation:
_____
_____
_____

What I'm grateful for today:
_____
_____
_____

What I'm doing today:
_____
_____
_____
_____
_____
_____
_____

What the Universe is doing:
_____
_____
_____
_____
_____
_____
_____

Biggest win of the day:
_____
_____
_____

Biggest lesson of the day:
_____
_____
_____

Date: ___/___/___

My Daily Intention:

My Affirmation:

What I'm grateful for today:

What I'm doing today:

What the Universe is doing:

Biggest win of the day:

Biggest lesson of the day:

THE DAILY JOURNAL

Date: _____ / _____ / _____

My Daily Intention:

My Affirmation:

What I'm grateful for today:

What I'm doing today:

What the Universe is doing:

Biggest win of the day:

Biggest lesson of the day:

Date: ___/___/___

My Daily Intention:

My Affirmation:

What I'm grateful for today:

What I'm doing today:

What the Universe is doing:

Biggest win of the day:

Biggest lesson of the day:

THE DAILY JOURNAL

Date: ____ / ____ / ____

My Daily Intention:
_____
_____
_____

My Affirmation:
_____
_____
_____

What I'm grateful for today:
_____
_____
_____

What I'm doing today:
_____
_____
_____
_____
_____
_____
_____

What the Universe is doing:
_____
_____
_____
_____
_____
_____
_____

Biggest win of the day:
_____
_____
_____

Biggest lesson of the day:
_____
_____
_____

Date: ____ / ____ / ____

My Daily Intention:

My Affirmation:

What I'm grateful for today:

What I'm doing today:

What the Universe is doing:

Biggest win of the day:

Biggest lesson of the day:

THE DAILY JOURNAL

Date: ___ / ___ / ___

My Daily Intention:
___

My Affirmation:
___

What I'm grateful for today:
___

What I'm doing today:
___

What the Universe is doing:
___

Biggest win of the day:
___

Biggest lesson of the day:
___

Date: ___/___/___

My Daily Intention:

My Affirmation:

What I'm grateful for today:

What I'm doing today:

What the Universe is doing:

Biggest win of the day:

Biggest lesson of the day:

THE DAILY JOURNAL

Date: ____ / ____ / ____

My Daily Intention:

My Affirmation:

What I'm grateful for today:

What I'm doing today:

What the Universe is doing:

Biggest win of the day:

Biggest lesson of the day:

Date: ___ / ___ / ___

My Daily Intention:

My Affirmation:

What I'm grateful for today:

What I'm doing today:

What the Universe is doing:

Biggest win of the day:

Biggest lesson of the day:

THE DAILY JOURNAL

Date: ____ / ____ / ____

My Daily Intention:
_____
_____
_____

My Affirmation:
_____
_____
_____

What I'm grateful for today:
_____
_____
_____

What I'm doing today:
_____
_____
_____
_____
_____
_____
_____

What the Universe is doing:
_____
_____
_____
_____
_____
_____
_____

Biggest win of the day:
_____
_____
_____

Biggest lesson of the day:
_____
_____
_____

Date: ___/___/___

My Daily Intention:

My Affirmation:

What I'm grateful for today:

What I'm doing today:

What the Universe is doing:

Biggest win of the day:

Biggest lesson of the day:

THE DAILY JOURNAL

Date: ____ / ____ / ____

My Daily Intention:

My Affirmation:

What I'm grateful for today:

What I'm doing today:

What the Universe is doing:

Biggest win of the day:

Biggest lesson of the day:

Date: ___/___/___

My Daily Intention:

My Affirmation:

What I'm grateful for today:

What I'm doing today:

What the Universe is doing:

Biggest win of the day:

Biggest lesson of the day:

THE DAILY JOURNAL

Date: ____ / ____ / ____

My Daily Intention:

My Affirmation:

What I'm grateful for today:

What I'm doing today:

What the Universe is doing:

Biggest win of the day:

Biggest lesson of the day:

Date: ____/____/____

My Daily Intention:

My Affirmation:

What I'm grateful for today:

What I'm doing today:

What the Universe is doing:

Biggest win of the day:

Biggest lesson of the day:

THE DAILY JOURNAL

Date: ____ / ____ / ____

My Daily Intention:
_____
_____
_____

My Affirmation:
_____
_____
_____

What I'm grateful for today:
_____
_____
_____

What I'm doing today:
_____
_____
_____
_____
_____
_____
_____

What the Universe is doing:
_____
_____
_____
_____
_____
_____
_____

Biggest win of the day:
_____
_____
_____

Biggest lesson of the day:
_____
_____
_____

Faith

Balancing the Crown Chakra

"Walk by faith, not by sight. As you take steps on faith, depending on Me, I will show you how much I can do for you. If you live your life too safely, you will never know the thrill of seeing Me work through you. When I gave you my spirit, I empowered you to live beyond your natural ability and strength. That's why it is so wrong to measure your energy level against the challenges ahead of you. The issue is not your strength, but Mine, which is limitless. By walking close to Me, you can accomplish My purposes in My strength."

- Sarah Young, Jesus Calling

- Does your mind find the negatives in a situation when something goes wrong? Reflect on the most positive person you know and describe their thought processes.

✧ Do your fears hinder you from following through with your desires? List every fear you currently have. Then reflect on and write down all of your strengths, successes, future opportunities and reasons for believing in yourself. Acknowledge which list is longer.

- Do you feel spiritually supported in this life? List the times you have felt guided and protected throughout your professional/personal adventures:

Date: ___ / ___ / ___

My Daily Intention:

My Affirmation:

What I'm grateful for today:

What I'm doing today:

What the Universe is doing:

Biggest win of the day:

Biggest lesson of the day:

THE DAILY JOURNAL

Date: /   /

My Daily Intention:

My Affirmation:

What I'm grateful for today:

What I'm doing today:

What the Universe is doing:

Biggest win of the day:

Biggest lesson of the day:

BALANCE AMONGST THE CHAOS

Date: ___ / ___ / ___

My Daily Intention:

My Affirmation:

What I'm grateful for today:

What I'm doing today:

What the Universe is doing:

Biggest win of the day:

Biggest lesson of the day:

THE DAILY JOURNAL

Date: ___ / ___ / ___

My Daily Intention:

My Affirmation:

What I'm grateful for today:

What I'm doing today:

What the Universe is doing:

Biggest win of the day:

Biggest lesson of the day:

BALANCE AMONGST THE CHAOS

Date: ___ / ___ / ___

My Daily Intention:

My Affirmation:

What I'm grateful for today:

What I'm doing today:

What the Universe is doing:

Biggest win of the day:

Biggest lesson of the day:

THE DAILY JOURNAL

Date: ___/___/___

My Daily Intention:

My Affirmation:

What I'm grateful for today:

What I'm doing today:

What the Universe is doing:

Biggest win of the day:

Biggest lesson of the day:

BALANCE AMONGST THE CHAOS

Date: /   /

My Daily Intention:

My Affirmation:

What I'm grateful for today:

What I'm doing today:

What the Universe is doing:

Biggest win of the day:

Biggest lesson of the day:

THE DAILY JOURNAL

Date: ___ / ___ / _____

My Daily Intention:

My Affirmation:

What I'm grateful for today:

What I'm doing today:

What the Universe is doing:

Biggest win of the day:

Biggest lesson of the day:

BALANCE AMONGST THE CHAOS

Date: __ / __ / __

My Daily Intention:

My Affirmation:

What I'm grateful for today:

What I'm doing today:

What the Universe is doing:

Biggest win of the day:

Biggest lesson of the day:

THE DAILY JOURNAL

Date: ____ / ____ / ____

My Daily Intention:

My Affirmation:

What I'm grateful for today:

What I'm doing today:

What the Universe is doing:

Biggest win of the day:

Biggest lesson of the day:

BALANCE AMONGST THE CHAOS

Date: ____ / ____ / ____

My Daily Intention:

My Affirmation:

What I'm grateful for today:

What I'm doing today:

What the Universe is doing:

Biggest win of the day:

Biggest lesson of the day:

THE DAILY JOURNAL

Date: ___ / ___ / ___

My Daily Intention:

My Affirmation:

What I'm grateful for today:

What I'm doing today:

What the Universe is doing:

Biggest win of the day:

Biggest lesson of the day:

Date: ___/___/___

My Daily Intention:

My Affirmation:

What I'm grateful for today:

What I'm doing today:

What the Universe is doing:

Biggest win of the day:

Biggest lesson of the day:

THE DAILY JOURNAL

Date: ___ / ___ / ___

My Daily Intention:

My Affirmation:

What I'm grateful for today:

What I'm doing today:

What the Universe is doing:

Biggest win of the day:

Biggest lesson of the day:

BALANCE AMONGST THE CHAOS

Date: ___ / ___ / ___

My Daily Intention:

My Affirmation:

What I'm grateful for today:

What I'm doing today:

What the Universe is doing:

Biggest win of the day:

Biggest lesson of the day:

THE DAILY JOURNAL

Date: ___ / ___ / ___

My Daily Intention:
_____
_____
_____

My Affirmation:
_____
_____
_____

What I'm grateful for today:
_____
_____
_____

What I'm doing today:
_____
_____
_____
_____
_____
_____

What the Universe is doing:
_____
_____
_____
_____
_____
_____

Biggest win of the day:
_____
_____
_____

Biggest lesson of the day:
_____
_____
_____

BALANCE AMONGST THE CHAOS

Date: ___ / ___ / ___

My Daily Intention:

My Affirmation:

What I'm grateful for today:

What I'm doing today:

What the Universe is doing:

Biggest win of the day:

Biggest lesson of the day:

THE DAILY JOURNAL

Date: /   /

My Daily Intention: My Affirmation:

What I'm grateful for today:

What I'm doing today: What the Universe is doing:

Biggest win of the day:

Biggest lesson of the day:

Date: ___/___/___

My Daily Intention:

My Affirmation:

What I'm grateful for today:

What I'm doing today:

What the Universe is doing:

Biggest win of the day:

Biggest lesson of the day:

THE DAILY JOURNAL

Date: ___ / ___ / ___

My Daily Intention:

My Affirmation:

What I'm grateful for today:

What I'm doing today:

What the Universe is doing:

Biggest win of the day:

Biggest lesson of the day:

BALANCE AMONGST THE CHAOS

Date: ___ / ___ / ___

My Daily Intention:

My Affirmation:

What I'm grateful for today:

What I'm doing today:

What the Universe is doing:

Biggest win of the day:

Biggest lesson of the day:

THE DAILY JOURNAL

Date: ___ / ___ / ___

My Daily Intention:

My Affirmation:

What I'm grateful for today:

What I'm doing today:

What the Universe is doing:

Biggest win of the day:

Biggest lesson of the day:

BALANCE AMONGST THE CHAOS

Date: ____ / ____ / ____

My Daily Intention:

My Affirmation:

What I'm grateful for today:

What I'm doing today:

What the Universe is doing:

Biggest win of the day:

Biggest lesson of the day:

THE DAILY JOURNAL

Date: ___ / ___ / ___

My Daily Intention:

My Affirmation:

What I'm grateful for today:

What I'm doing today:

What the Universe is doing:

Biggest win of the day:

Biggest lesson of the day:

BALANCE AMONGST THE CHAOS

Date: ___ / ___ / ___

My Daily Intention:

My Affirmation:

What I'm grateful for today:

What I'm doing today:

What the Universe is doing:

Biggest win of the day:

Biggest lesson of the day:

THE DAILY JOURNAL

Date: /   /

My Daily Intention:

My Affirmation:

What I'm grateful for today:

What I'm doing today:

What the Universe is doing:

Biggest win of the day:

Biggest lesson of the day:

BALANCE AMONGST THE CHAOS

Date: ___ / ___ / ___

My Daily Intention:

My Affirmation:

What I'm grateful for today:

What I'm doing today:

What the Universe is doing:

Biggest win of the day:

Biggest lesson of the day:

THE DAILY JOURNAL

Date: ___ / ___ / ___

My Daily Intention:

My Affirmation:

What I'm grateful for today:

What I'm doing today:

What the Universe is doing:

Biggest win of the day:

Biggest lesson of the day:

BALANCE AMONGST THE CHAOS

Date: ___ / ___ / _____

My Daily Intention:

My Affirmation:

What I'm grateful for today:

What I'm doing today:

What the Universe is doing:

Biggest win of the day:

Biggest lesson of the day:

THE DAILY JOURNAL

Date: ___ / ___ / ____

My Daily Intention:

My Affirmation:

What I'm grateful for today:

What I'm doing today:

What the Universe is doing:

Biggest win of the day:

Biggest lesson of the day:

Closing Letter from the Author

My dear friend, you have used all the pages of this daily journal. This book is now completely yours. It is filled with your aspirations, intentions, finished to-do lists, daily wins, and personal reflections you have carried through your days and every milestone as of late. Maybe you finished it in a year, maybe 18 months, or maybe you started writing in this journal two years ago. Do not stress. The time it took to complete this book is irrelevant — there is no need to rush through any element of self-growth. Time is an illusion and being in a hurry to improve yourself or complete a goal only slows down the process.

Although you have finished this journal, your journey of self-improvement is not over and is truly just beginning. Now would be a timely moment to reflect on every minor and major milestone since starting this journal. Review the biggest lessons and wins of each day, any manifestations that have come to fruition, and the goals you have accomplished. Compare your behaviors, daily habits, energy levels, and perspective on life to how you used to be and to others around you. Comparison is crucial for self-mastery and personal growth. Assess your lifestyle, behaviors, and self-talk compared to your previous habits and how you no longer participate in them. Acknowledge any personal growth and the shift in your mindset as you have begun actively working on yourself.

It is natural and quite acceptable to compare yourself to others. Frankly, comparison can be a very beneficial tool for measuring your progress and planning how to evolve going forward. Do not compare yourself to your friends and family with a judgmental attitude or with an underlying condescending manner. However, contrasting your behaviors to others' can be a powerful tool for measuring your own growth. Notice your old habits or seemingly negative behaviors in others. Maybe you

THE DAILY JOURNAL

notice a negative behavior or toxic trait in a friend or a co-worker you used to actively partake in. Simply observing how others behave is a great measurement of your own progress.

Going forward, find positive behaviors in others that you wish to mirror and manifest for yourself. Perhaps you desire to adopt the disciplined work ethic of your co-worker, your personal trainer's dedication to fitness, your best friend's ability to unbiasedly listen to others, or the confident manner in which your manager carries themself. Find others who challenge you personally, financially, athletically, or professionally. Use their journeys as inspiration for where you would like to go next in your life. Open your eyes and ears and admire the positive qualities of others. Use these as a guide to building an even better, stronger, and happier version of yourself. The things you admire about others are what you truly desire for yourself. Use this inspiration to motivate your next milestone and new intentions. Self-mastery, reflection, comparison, and planning are crucial elements in building the roadmap of your life.

Have faith and trust you are on your right path. How do you know you're on the correct path, you ask? Simple. You feel good. You're feeling a little bit better each day. You're making minor adjustments to your lifestyle/mindset and you can start to feel some positive changes. That's when you know you're doing exactly what you should be doing. When you feel fulfilled physically, emotionally, mentally, and professionally, it's called alignment. You're congruent with your morals/higher purpose and agree with all parts of your life.

It is possible, it is worth the work, and most importantly: it can be truly enjoyable. Don't forget to be gentle with yourself, laugh really hard and find joy in the little things along the way. The happier you are, the happier your community becomes. Stay bright and spread your light.

One Last Thing...

I would love to hear all of the successful milestones, breakthroughs, revelations, and manifestations that happen for you during your time using this journal. Nothing makes me happier than hearing the successful moments that occur when incorporating spirituality and mindfulness practices into your days, taking accountability for your daily habits, and building a lifestyle you aspire to have. I collect and study all kinds of success stories: large, small, professional, emotional, romantic, financial or otherwise. Please feel welcomed to share any highs and lows with me as well as any inquisitions you may have.

Peace & Blessings,

Sarah Iaccarino
www.healwithaligntherapies.com
aligntherapies.llc@gmail.com

www.ingramcontent.com/pod-product-compliance
Lightning Source LLC
Chambersburg PA
CBHW041306240426
43661CB00011B/1035